The Truth About Trees

poems

by Charles Ghigna

The Truth About Trees

poems

by Charles Ghigna

Negative Capability Press • Mobile, Alabama

THE TRUTH ABOUT TREES
poems by Charles Ghigna

Negative Capability Press
negativecapabilitypress.org

Library of Congress Control Number: 2021943839
PAPERBACK ISBN: 978-1-7345902-8-9
HARDCOVER ISBN: 978-1-7345902-6-5
EBOOK ISBN: 978-1-7345902-9-6

Cover art by Chip Ghigna
Book design by Miles Parsons

to Chip Ghigna,
for all your love & inspiration

for Debra,
always

"If you trust in Nature, in the small Things that hardly anyone sees
and that can so suddenly become huge, immeasurable;
if you have this love for what is humble and try very simply,
as someone who serves, to win the confidence of what seems poor:
then everything will become easier for you, more coherent and
somehow more reconciling, not in your conscious mind perhaps,
which stays behind, astonished, but in your innermost awareness,
awakeness, and knowledge."

—Rainier Maria Rilke

Contents

I

II

III

IV

V

I

The Truth About Trees

Forget the metaphors,
the silent sentinels,
the branches of life,

the truth about trees
does not live in a poem,
it lives deep in the forest,

in the quiet of the morning light,
in the shadows they cast
across your face.

Touch one.
Feel its strength
beneath your fingertips.

Stand barefoot before it.
Feel its energy rising
from the roots.

Listen to it breathe.
Look up into
its canopy of leaves.

Let its majestic silence
settle over you,
settle into you,

until you and tree are one,
until you begin to know
its meaning,

until you begin to know
the truth
about trees.

Treescape

Stare into the face of Nature
Till the forest owns your eyes.
Search beneath the surface shine
Until her depth dispels your lies.

Climb your stare upon her trees
Until you see all shades of green.
Cast your vision past itself
Until your sight becomes the scene.

The Elms

The elms here are easy to talk about,
though we never really take them one at a time,
never really know one with words.

Maybe our eyes are the problem,
and when we are close, our hands, too,
get in the way.

We almost cannot walk by an elm
with our fingers still in our pockets,
and I wonder if it is their silence

that we want each time to touch
or simply the feel of something stronger
than ourselves, something rooted and solid

that may tell the truth on us
whenever we come out of our pockets
and open our eyes.

Nature Trail

These weathered steps
hand-cut
from old railroad ties
lead us down
past the stump bench
to the stream
that flows
from the top
of the hill
and winds us
past dogwood
poplar and pine
where we pause
to listen
to the wind
in the trees
to the babble
of the brook
that calls
us home.

Ever Green

Down, down, down again I go
Into the hollows of the deep green forest,
Into the untrodden damp green forest
Where only soiled boot soles know

How cool green mornings can be,
How soily sweet the mud,
How slippery fresh each step,
Step, step beneath the ever tree.

Oak

Like the steady face
of the flying squirrel,
we sail through the parting air

of falling leaves
and land at last
on the forest floor.

We scamper here and there
searching for the perfect acorn,
that little balm of time

that holds the tree of life
within its tiny seed,
that tempting core

we want so much to find,
that piece of us
we want so much to be.

Suddenly September

A crisp cool
sky blue
lazy day
in the middle
of summer
and suddenly
the leaves
shimmer
with a golden secret
and the breeze
whispers low
"It's autumn."

October

Haiku

Artist autumn comes,
paints her blush across each tree,
drops palette, and leaves.

Autumn Leaves

In their yellow-most goings,
leaves of maple
ride breezes to the ground.
You can hear their sound
each autumn afternoon
as the crisp air cuts
through the trees
and hurries us along
the golden sidewalks
home.

The Cold Gray Days of Winter

In the cold gray days of winter
When the sky turns iron blue
And the leafless trees stand silent
With nothing left to do,

There comes a cry across the land
That carries seeds of spring,
The echo of the distant hawk,
The sun upon his wing.

If I Were Robert Frost

I'd pray that my soft words
would fall like snow,
blank white verse
upon the countryside
of your heart,
would fill the forest
of your dreams with light
and quietly lead you
through the trees
back to our own
endless road
not taken.

Buck Dancing

Two eight-point buck
lay beside the frozen lake,
their antlers locked
in a last dance.

It was their rite
to fight for dominance
in this, their final
rutting season,

to die for the doe
they will never know.
This is the hunting season
when boys search through the cold

for the buck that will make them a man.
This is the season they will find
by the lake their future
frozen for a moment in the snow.

Before We Lived

Before we lived
Behind window door.
Before we counted
Seasons four.

Before we prayed
To a hallowed heaven.
Before we counted
Days by seven.

Before the suits
And argyle socks.
Before the calendars
And broken clocks.

Life was a journey
With freedom to roam.
Time was a river
That flowed on its own.

A River of Stars

Study the river at night.
Find your reflection in a star.
You are a star in the river.

Shining, flowing,
constant as the current
that pulls toward the sea,

toward the shore
of time and space,
now and forever,

one river without end,
one constant river
that carries your star

over ancient stones
that polish
with your passing,

stones round and shining
like a star in the river
of you.

Think Like a River

Think like a river.
Dream like the sky.
Drift like an eagle
That circles on high.

Breathe like the wind
That calls from the trees.
Ride like a wave
That caresses the seas.

Sleep like a secret
That whispers the night.
Wake like a wish
That warms you with light.

Obeying Stones

The earth accepts what rock must give in rain.
There is no law for this. It was before
the matriarch worshipped the sun,

before the patriarch hid inside the moon,
before we carved a cradle from the tree
and sent it rocking to the stars.

We now sow our forests into straighter rows,
measure each new seedling's worth with care
as though it grows for us and not itself.

We build stone walls around each countryside
and weigh each field with tombs to mark our past,
then pause to watch the season's final hare

spring from her yellow hutch to cross our path,
till somewhere just beyond our sight she stops,
turns to us, then runs the other way.

Her colors hint of every sign for snow,
that piece of fur from which we cut our cloth.
But we must search beyond the field for what we need

to where the mountains point above the coming clouds,
to the vast gray slate of birdless sky
where we will mark our future in the stone.

III

Aries Sideshow

Like a magnet
under the magician's table,
the swan's reflection
pulls her across the lake,

while deep inside the brush
an unseen hand
pulls rabbits
out of rabbits.

Spring Cleaning

First signs of life
and we stand in a bed of weeds
pulling up wild vines in the sun.

The honeysuckle holds
tight to the house,
bracing itself against the red brick,

but we have come for it all,
we have come to clear the way,
marching side by side into spring,

into this season that pulls us out
of ourselves and lets us hold life
in our hands by the roots.

Spring Mountain

Spring Mountain,
a waking giant,
grabs at April's clouds.

Come see his
piney fingers
touch the sky.

Trees of Fire

The trees have held their tongues too long.
Tonight they sing a dying song.
Crackle hiss sizzle pop
Ashes soaring to the top.

Yellow red orange cry
Confessing secrets to the sky.
Rings of trees. Rings of fire.
Rings of flame soaring higher.

Past the mast of sailing clouds.
Past the echoed cry of crowds.
Past the last sad wisp of pine.
Hear them whistle. Hear them whine.

Respect the Fire

Respect the fire.
It has no conscience,
though its tortured soul
aspires to brighter heights,
leaping, lapping,
swaying, crackling,
climbing upon itself
out of the forest of hell
toward heaven,
past the moon and sun
in search of a sanctity of stars.

The Shape of Life

Do not think only of the circle of life
as the arc from birth to death.
Think of the circle of life as the shape
that forms the image of our lives,
that roundness forever around us.

Our home, the Earth, is a circle.
Our life-force light, the Sun.
Our night light, the Moon.
Our first sight, wondrous and wise,
the circles of our mother's eyes.

Nature loves her circles.
The eye of the flower,
The rings of the tree,
The stone-tossed ripples of lake,
The apple, the orange, the grape.

The dandelion and the bubble
that float on the summer air,
then light on the rush of water
to ride the tide down the drain.
The final circle, a drop of rain.

On Edge

Look again.
It is not the tree you want to see.
It is the edge of its leaves you desire,
the clean, clear sharpness of light,
the unbroken final line that surrounds us,
the perfect, outer edge of our lives.

Our eyes are lies.
We cannot see what is in front of us.
It is only the outline of our lives that is true.
It is there we come to find meaning,
that which defines what we hold so dear inside,
there on the outer edge where there is no room for error.

The Edge of the Universe

The newly discovered galaxy 4C41.7
is 15 billion light years from Earth which
is about 90 percent the distance to what is
thought to be the edge of the universe.

                                    --AP report

What is it that awaits us
in this distant, unknown place
that begins at the edge
of our outer most thoughts,
this place that pulls us
out of this world,
out of our minds,
and sends us into orbit
in search of answers
to more than our mere universe?

Whatever we may discover,
whatever we may lose or find,
we now know there is a place
that we have only seen
inside our deepest thoughts,
an endless other place
where truth plays hide and seek
and lets us know that we are but
a small beginning, a simple other side
of some other outer edge.

Winter Forest

We march into the gray dawn
feeling older than our bones
that hold onto their sleep
like grazing, aged cattle
waiting, eyes closed to the wind,
on a winter, slaughter morning.
We search through the fog for a sign,
for the coming sun to burn the way,
to lead us to the rainbow bridge,
to keep us from this cattle call.

IV

Over Herd

This time it will be different.
This time we will not go
like our bovine brothers

one by one down the ramp,
head first through the chute
into the slaughterhouse,

into the waiting slug of night.
This time we will rouse the herd,
we will rise from our dung

drenched funeral boards,
we will sway from side to side
in our heavy wave of defiance,

we will dance our rite to life,
we will rock and roll this cattle car
right off its clacking tracks.

Brave New Whirl

We drift in a nether world
between now and then
where time is a river

that drowns the night,
where memory purls easy over ice
and rocks our lies to sleep,

where slices of truth, ripe as morning,
sit on the salty edge
of every brave new whirl.

Day Dream

Childhood,
and again
we are outside

on a hilltop
staring up
at the clouds

searching past the cumulus
for the long-tail dragons
and silver sailing ships

that have come to take us away
to this rare dream
of dreaming.

Field Trip

Sunday, and we drive past the last building
to where its shadow no longer touches the car.
We stare at the broken line until it becomes earth

and listen to the crickets when we stop.
We join them in their singing, filling
our lungs with pine and magnolia.

We lie down in a bed of clover
and watch the moon on its way to morning.
We sleep until the sun warms our dreams,

until the firm hand of a friendly farmer
helps us back to our feet, until the trust
of his grip sends us on our way home

to the buildings, to the shadows,
to the broken yellow line
that sent us searching for this field.

Going All the Way

It is an afternoon in mid July
when we finally do the dare,
run full-tilt across the field,

close our eyes, leap into the sky—
and we are up and over the shadows,
above the weight of summer's heat,

flying like we've always dreamed of doing,
arms stretched out into wings,
hair blown back in waves of silk,

rising and falling and rising again,
freer than we have ever been,
wishing we could bring back to earth

what we have known in dreams,
in all those times like this
before we learned to trust our eyes.

Black Oranges

On a sand dune in the middle of nowhere north of Orlando,
I stumble into an unfinished concrete block house of broken windows
sitting abandoned in the back of a gone-dry orange grove.

On the interstate below, a line of cars snakes its way home.
The distant hiss from a passing plane bound for Miami
loses its voice inside the last cloud of this August afternoon.

The heavy sun sinks into the hilly knee-deep sands
leaving a cast of shadows from the gnarled trees,
sad sculptures stoned to death by the unforgiving heat.

A sea of black oranges lie half-buried in the hot sand.
Unpicked by their forgotten pickers they grow
into balls of pitch beneath their shadeless trees.

Inside the block house shards liter the cement floor.
Rust clings to a doorless hinge. Nothing moves,
creaks, cries on this hill, this grove, this house.

A fading photo nailed to the gray wall stares out at us,
a family portrait, a wash of drowned faces who lost their way
in this hellacious sea of endless sand.

Rain

A rumble of morning thunder
my only companion,
I stick my arms out the window
and gather raindrops in my hands.

I baptize myself in a flash of lightning,
my warm breath turning
the broken window pane into a mirror,
turning me into a ghost,

into this stranger
who holds rain in his hands
like a beggar, like a thief,
like a priest without mercy or shame.

Optical Allusion

Like the baby who first
sees himself in the mirror
and thinks he has met a stranger,

we shuffle through old photographs
searching for the one we used to be.
But no matter how many times we smiled,

no matter how many times
we combed our hair and acted coy,
no matter how many times

the camera made us small,
we can only guess the fate
of this smiling, young stranger

who once resembled us,
this smiling, young stranger
we hold like a fortune in our hands.

Signs

I am the back of the attic mirror.
From my side I see only out.
The change of seasons I once wore
leaves no reflection on me.

I wear my silver fleck in pieces
like the holey No Hunting sign
aired by the bully's bullets.
The wind whistles through, not at, me.

A parade of pale faces drives by
searching for the one with the reckless gun.
But they will not find me in this town
for I am attic bound.

My lead hides in the grass a mile away.
My shell rusts in the weeds by the road.
I am attic faced in shadows.
I search through the dark for a sign.

The House on the Cliff by the Sea

I come Ishmael to you from the midnight sea.
The gray fog clings, a pasted beard, to my cheeks.
It grows wild from my chin around the world.

You raise the lantern
higher to your face
and stare into the dark at a dream.

The window holds you
like a portrait hung against the sky.
I come bringing morning in my beard.

Peace Talks

Open, except for our eyes,
we lie flat on our backs
studying our separate darknesses,

re-traveling the two steep roads
that brought us to this place
of all-night promises

where we make up endless stories
that we could tell each other
if we should ever forget ourselves,

break this silence, open our eyes,
and make love to this two-faced stranger
called us.

Chess Life

This game is too glib,
too easy to make
into a metaphor for life,

too simple to say
these are the squares we live,
these are the moves we make,

too superficial to suggest
we must sacrifice ourselves
to check another mate,

too unnecessary to speak
the unspoken rule
of moving within our own time,

too trite to tell
how we must play in patterns
and never out of turn,

too self-conscious to say
how after we pawn to the top
we may move wherever we wish,

too realistic to write
this cunning board game
could be but a gamut of life.

Cell Fish

Like fish in a bowl
We're losing our soul
Swimming in circles
And going to cell.

Glassy eyed
And looking down
Searching for all
That we never found.

A text,
A tweet,
We pic what we eat,
Our egos begging for likes.

An instagram,
A thank you ma'm,
A clever meme
With a rhyme.

We hold in our hand
The glass in the sand
That's running away
With our time.

Tell Me

about how you lost
your interest
in words,

about how you feel
so full
of them

you think you might
break out
in red letters,

think if you hear
another one
you will scream,

will run blindly
into the woods
and hide,

will dip your finger
into the stream
and write your final line,

will lie on your back
and stare up
at the stars,

will run home
through the dark
and sit alone by the fire

until someone who cares
comes to your side and says
"tell me."

A Prayer for Planet Earth

Beyond the cry
Of verdant birth,
Beyond the edge
Of Mother Earth,

Sweet Universe
Of starry skies,
Cool our hearts,
Burn our lies.

Heal our spirits,
Father Sun.
Save our planet.
Make us One.

Little Spaces

Little spaces.
Tiny traces.
That's what
I look for.

Shady spots.
Small clay pots.
Garden walls
Without a door.

Hiding places
With no faces
Where the world
Cannot find me.

In my tree house
Like a free mouse—
That's where I most
Want to be.

Be Still

Be still in the world wherever you are,
listen to life's lullaby;
the heartbeat, the breathing, the giving, receiving,
the sun and the moon and the star.

They all shine true through the essence of you,
a beacon of boundless light;
the father, the mother, the sister, the brother,
all are within you tonight.

Let the flow of the seas, the lilt of the breeze,
the rush and the calm of all time
carry your dreams along rivers and streams
and let you be still where you are.

Night Trees

Trees of night,
we stand apart
in the silent darkness
waiting for dawn
to warm us back
into the light of day
with whispers
of morning
that will tell
the truth on us,
that will reveal
the secret
of how we are
rooted together,
connected
to each other
in this forest
of forgiveness.

Charles Ghigna lives in a treehouse in the middle of Alabama. He is the author of more than 100 books from Random House, Disney, Scholastic, Simon & Schuster, Time Inc. and other publishers. He has written more than 5,000 poems for children and adults that appear in anthologies, newspapers, and magazines ranging from *The New Yorker* and *Harper's* to *Highlights* and *Cricket* magazines. He served as poet-in-residence and chair of creative writing at the Alabama School of Fine Arts, instructor of creative writing at Samford University, poetry editor of *English Journal* for the National Council of Teachers of English, and as a nationally syndicated feature writer for Tribune Media Services. He speaks at schools, conferences, libraries, and literary events throughout the U.S. and overseas, and has read his poems at The Library of Congress, The John F. Kennedy Center, American Library in Paris, American School in Paris, and the International Schools of South America. For more information, visit his website at CharlesGhigna.com